A Citizen's Guide to
Law & Order

Heinemann
LIBRARY

Paul Wignall

www.heinemann.co.uk/library
visit our website to find out more information about **Heinemann Library** books.

To order:
 Phone 44 (0) 1865 888066

 Send a fax to 44 (0) 1865 314091

Visit the Heinemann Bookshop at www.heinemann.co.uk/library to browse our catalogue and order online.

First published in Great Britain by Heinemann Library, Halley Court, Jordan Hill, Oxford OX2 8EJ,
a division of Reed Educational and Professional Publishing Ltd.

Heinemann is a registered trademark of Reed Educational & Professional Publishing Limited.

OXFORD MELBOURNE AUCKLAND JOHANNESBURG BLANTYRE GABORONE IBADAN PORTSMOUTH NH (USA) CHICAGO

© Reed Educational and Professional Publishing Ltd 2002
The moral right of the proprietor has been asserted.

Designed by M2 Graphic Design
Indexed by Indexing Specialists
Originated by Ambassador Litho Ltd
Printed in Hong Kong/China

06 05 04 03 02
10 9 8 7 6 5 4 3 2 1

ISBN 0 431 14495 8

British Library Cataloguing in Publication Data
Wignall, Paul
A citizen's guide to law and order
1. Law – Great Britain – Juvenile literature
2. Police – Great Britain – Juvenile literature
I. Title II.Law and order
349.4'1

Acknowledgements
The Publishers would like to thank the following for permission to reproduce photgraphs:
AKG London p24; Burghley House Collection/Bridgeman Art library p8; Courtesy of the Court of Justice of the European Communities p23; David Hoffman Photo
Library p32; Getty Images/Jonathon Morgan pp5, 42; Mark Harvey/ID8 p35; © Historical Picture Archive/Corbis p18; © Hulton-Deutsch Collection/Corbis p11;
The Louvre, Bridgeman Art Library/Peter Willis p6; Stewart Mark/Camera Press p29; Eric C Owens/California Department of Corrections p36; PA Photos pp38, 40;
Popperfoto/Reuters p12; Rex Features Ltd p30; © Gustavo Tomsich/Corbis p26; Universal Pictorial Press pp16, 20.

Cover photograph reproduced with permission of Associated Press.

Every effort has been made to contact copyright holders of any material reproduced in this book.
Any omissions will be rectified in subsequent printings if notice is given to the Publisher.

CONTENTS

Any words appearing in the text in bold, **like this**, are explained in the Glossary.

INTRODUCTION
Law, order, justice and you

Laura's story

When Laura was eight, her mother's new boyfriend, Rob, started to live with them. It wasn't long before Laura began to hear shouts and screams after she had gone to bed, which scared her. But one day she got up and went downstairs. Rob was hitting her mother. Laura tried to push him away, but he got hold of her and hit her, too. That was when her mother picked Laura up and ran out of the house and into the house next door. Laura heard a lot more noise and shouting, then everything went quiet. She looked outside and saw a police car, and a policeman putting Rob into the back. Then a policewoman came and talked to her and her mother. Now Rob isn't allowed near their house and her mother has a special telephone she can use to call the police in case Rob tries to come back. That makes Laura feel a lot safer.

Duane's story

Duane knew it was stupid and wrong, but he let his friend Alex persuade him to go into the shop and, when the woman behind the counter wasn't looking, to put the bars of chocolate in his pocket. He was walking back to Alex when a hand grabbed his shoulder. The next thing he knew, he was in the back room of the shop. There was a policeman there and on the table was a TV monitor. They were watching a video recording of Duane stealing the chocolate. Duane started to cry when the policeman asked for his name and address and told him he'd have to go to the police station to answer questions.

Polly's story

It was like war! Every time they tried to get into their drive with the car, they found their neighbours' motorbike blocking the way. Polly's dad had asked them to move it, but they never did. Then things started getting worse. They found rubbish thrown over the fence – old food, papers, cans and worse. Then the dog started coming into the garden, digging up the flowerbeds and messing everywhere. In the end they had to get the council in, and a **solicitor**. Not that it's perfect now, but at least they get some peace.

The law affects us in many different ways. Some of them are obvious, like the examples you've just read. We know that if we do something wrong, we are likely to be dealt with by the police, and may have to go to court. The police are also there to protect us, from physical cruelty or from our property being stolen.

There are other laws, not so obvious at first, but just as important. There are laws about employment, about going to school, or about paying taxes to the government. There are laws to control the safety of medicines, to protect animals from cruelty, and to control how goods and services are advertised and sold.

There are also laws that affect the way in which countries behave towards one another – international laws about trade, **immigration** and spying, for example. There are laws about the sea and there are even laws about the human use of outer space!

In this book we will see how the law can be used to:

>> Settle disputes

>> Protect vulnerable people and property

>> Punish wrongdoers

>> Control and order our lives in society.

What is justice?

On the top of the Old Bailey, the central criminal law court in London, there is a statue of 'Justice'. She has a sword in her hand, to show how the law is strong, can punish and can protect. But **Justice** is often also shown as blindfolded. This is a way of saying that the law should be blind – it shouldn't favour one person or another in a dispute just because that person may be rich or powerful. The job of the law is to do what is right.

Many people worry that the law is too often used not to protect the weak, but to give even more power to the strong. The law can seem overpowering and impersonal; it's what 'they' do to 'us'. Certainly, the law can be used by people in positions of power to control others, but it can also be used to limit the power of governments or big businesses. The statue of Justice holds a sword with two sharp edges – it can be used for good or for bad; how it is actually used depends on us.

The statue of Justice on the top of the Central Criminal Court (the 'Old Bailey') in London.

THE LAW THROUGH HISTORY
Revenge and duty

Revenge has always been a favourite theme of playwrights and filmmakers. The idea of revenge suggests that law does not exist, or at least depends upon the belief that only the family of a wronged person has the duty to put right that wrong. The idea of the 'blood feud' (that a family's honour is shamed until the enemy's blood is spilled) lies behind William Shakespeare's Hamlet, as well as the most ancient plays of classical Greece, Aeschylus' trilogy, *Oresteia*. These plays can tell us a lot about how people felt about the law in ancient Greece. Many aspects of the laws of the Greeks are still important today.

Aeschylus' three plays tell the story of two generations of the family of Atreus. King Agamemnon has returned from success in the Trojan war, only to be killed by his wife Clytemnestra in revenge for the death of their daughter, Iphigenia, whom Agamemnon sacrificed at the start of the war. His surviving children, Electra and Orestes, vow to kill their mother. When Orestes has murdered Clytemnestra, he is pursued by three avenging goddesses, The Furies, who are determined to kill him in turn. Eventually Orestes is put on trial in Athens. He is released only after the god Apollo and the goddess Athene plead for him. They argue, successfully but for us controversially, that Orestes was justified in avenging his father's death by killing his mother, because the **rights** of fathers are greater than the rights of mothers.

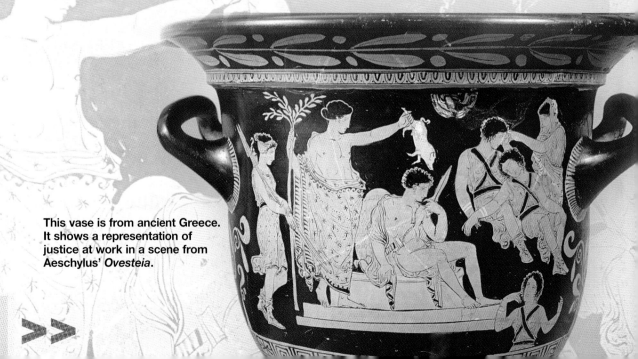

This vase is from ancient Greece. It shows a representation of justice at work in a scene from Aeschylus' *Ovesteia*.

We may feel that this is not a very good answer. But the end of the *Oresteia* does make it clear that revenge cannot go on forever; there needs to be a control over a family feud or **vendetta**. Aeschylus' solution has three elements that have continued to be very important for law, and for discussions of right and wrong behaviour.

A higher authority

First of all, the gods present the arguments for and against Orestes. There is a sense that the only way to resolve disputes that may otherwise go on for generations is by turning to an authority figure, who will create laws controlling people's behaviour and have the power to enforce them. There have been many such law codes about all aspects of life: the Ten Commandments, which have had an enormous influence on Judaism, Christianity and Islam, are a very old example. People believe these laws are the commandments of God, and so they have greater power and authority.

The power of argument

Aeschylus' second point is to have Apollo and Athene, the gods, arguing about what should happen to Orestes, and presenting their views in very persuasive language. Legal decisions are greatly influenced by the use of language, which has the power to persuade people. The art of rhetoric (persuasive speech) is extremely important in the law. We still find it used today by **barristers** and **solicitors**, arguing on behalf of clients or **defendants** in British courts. Sometimes there are concerns that the law is more about who can be the most persuasive, rather than about actually finding out what happened. This worry is as old as the courts of law.

Trial by jury

Finally, Aeschylus describes the trial of Orestes. The Furies want him to be put to death. Apollo defends him. However, at the end of the play, Aeschylus shows the people of Athens, the **jury**, deciding what will happen to Orestes. They vote in his favour, following the authority of the god Apollo.

The idea that someone should be tried by his or her fellow citizens, so important in ancient Athens, has become a crucial part of our own legal system. Not only juries, a randomly selected group of twelve people, but also **magistrates**, who have some legal training but are not professional **lawyers**, are given the power to make decisions in law courts. Laws may be handed down by people in power, but decisions about guilt and innocence, and about how someone should be punished, are often made by our fellow citizens, who have listened to the arguments and have made up their own minds.

THE LAW THROUGH HISTORY
Punishment, forgiveness and reconciliation

The law is a long list of dos and don'ts. It tells us how we are allowed to behave, and it limits what we do in order to protect others (it also, of course, limits what others can do in order to protect us). The law is also a system of **sanctions**: it limits behaviour and it protects us by making it clear that there are consequences to what we do. If we break the law, we are likely to pay the penalty.

Thomas Hobbes (1588–1679) wrote a theory of law in his book *Leviathan*.

The rule of law

The seventeenth-century English writer Thomas Hobbes came to the conclusion that it was only the strength of law that prevented society from collapsing into violence and disorder. Hobbes was writing at the time when Britain was in the middle of civil war. King Charles I had been executed by **Parliament**, and it was no longer clear how the law could operate to protect citizens. In his book *Leviathan*, Hobbes spoke of human life as 'nasty, poor, brutish and short', and argued that only the **rule of law** could protect people and property.

He argued that laws are essentially rules laid down by an authority that also has the power to make sure those rules are kept, and to punish those who break them. These rules might come from all the decisions that **judges** have made in the past (this is called **case law**) or they might come from specific rules and laws discussed and agreed upon by a person or a group of people. Laws might be commands of a single person of supreme power – a king or queen – or they might be the result of detailed discussion and agreement by a group of appointed or elected representatives, such as Parliament. This is called 'primary **legislation**'.

Good laws

For Hobbes, one of the most important things was that laws should not benefit one group over another. Laws should be rational: it should be possible to show that they are good rules – and they should apply equally to everyone.

Hobbes makes a third, very important point. He stresses that the law is only concerned with a person's intentions. People are able to make decisions about what they will do, and legal sanctions are only to be applied when people deliberately break the law.

A lot hangs on this idea. Some argue that people who do not understand the difference between right and wrong, or between what the law allows and what the law does not allow, should not be punished if their actions somehow break the law. So, very young children, or people with some severe mental health problems may be treated differently from adults who can make free and conscious decisions.

What is punishment for?

Thomas Hobbes thought that the law punished wrongdoers for committing a crime, and also in order to stop others from committing similar crimes in the future. In other words, a criminal should be made to pay for what he or she had done. It was also hoped that other people would think twice before committing a criminal act in the future when they saw what happens when a law is broken.

Since Hobbes' day, a completely different view has sometimes been presented – that there are times when the law should aim less for punishment, and more for forgiveness and reconciliation. This view argues that punishment hardly ever works because it depends on the idea that we are completely free agents when we do something wrong. But we are always affected by our position in society, and by our upbringing. We may even be affected by our genes. There is also evidence that punishment does not prevent a person from offending again and rarely stops others from committing crimes. So, some people argue that the duty of the state is to recognize that a person's behaviour can only be changed by helping that person to understand what he or she has done, and to feel sorry for his or her actions. Should we therefore put most of our efforts into helping people to change their behaviour, rather then imprisoning them?

FIND OUT...

Do you think that it's possible to help lawbreakers to behave differently? Or do you think there still needs to be some element of retribution (making people 'pay' for what they've done)? Do you think that punishing someone ever stops someone else from committing a crime? Have a look in your local newspaper to see what punishments are handed out for different crimes. Which, in your view, are fair and which are unfair?

THE LAW THROUGH HISTORY
Human rights

What is **justice**? Some people say that it is 'doing what the law requires' – in other words, obeying the laws of the land. But other people think that laws are too often made in favour of powerful individuals or groups, and that 'justice' can only come about by limiting the power of the law. In other words, laws may actually create inequalities and **oppression**, and there needs to be a balance to bring about **equality** and freedom.

Four steps on the path towards human rights

In 1215, some of the leading landowners of England rebelled against their king, John. They believed that he had been misusing his royal power. These landowners soon defeated John, and on 15 June, at Runnymede, an island on the River Thames, they made him sign an agreement that effectively limited his power. This Magna Carta (Latin for 'Great Charter') included an agreement that no one should in future be imprisoned without a trial, and that any attempts by the king to raise money should first receive the agreement of the landowners themselves. The Magna Carta is often seen as a first step on the road to **human rights**. Although it was little more than a power-sharing agreement in favour of a small group of rich landowners,

it paved the way for the growth of parliaments centuries later, and towards greater equality under the law.

Bartolomeo de las Casas

In 1550 the Spanish invasion of the Americas was in full swing, with the **indigenous** peoples being conquered, and often slaughtered, in the search for gold. In April of that year, King Charles V called a halt to the invasion and demanded a debate about the morality of what was taking place. When the debate opened in the Spanish city of Valladolid, a theologian called Sepulveda argued that the peoples of America were 'slaves by nature' and 'inferior beings' – indeed were hardly human at all. Sepulveda had never been to the Americas, but his opponent Bartolomeo de las Casas had, and he spoke out against the viciousness of the Spanish invasion. Las Casas went further in his defence of the indigenous peoples. He spoke of the basic humanity of 'all the peoples of the world' - that all people 'are alike' and should be treated with equal respect. Las Casas so impressed his hearers that he won the debate, but it didn't stop the invasion of the Americas. However, his voice remains a crucial one in the history of human rights.

The United States Declaration of Independence

In 1776, the United States of America declared its independence from Britain, and issued a declaration proclaiming that 'all men are created equal…and…endowed with certain rights… including…life, liberty and the pursuit of happiness'. Although this declaration was a most important step in the development of human rights, the reality was that it was made by a country still engaged in the slave trade, still destroying the culture of Native Americans, and the people themselves. Neither did it make any mention of the rights of women to equal treatment and opportunity. But the Declaration of Independence has acted as a focus for groups that seek equality of treatment under the law, and who want to fight for their own freedom.

The Universal Declaration of Human Rights

In 1948, the United Nations drew up a charter of human rights that was intended to protect the rights of all human beings.

The attempted destruction of the Jewish people by Nazi Germany had given a strong reason for this declaration to be created, and although, like the United States' declaration of 1776, it is often broken, it demonstrates support for human rights. In fact, it has been a major factor in the growth of human rights throughout the world.

Some people doubt that a charter of human rights is of any importance. They point to the continued presence of **slavery**, oppression and **inequality** in the world, and doubt that such declarations really do any good. But others argue that the basis of true justice is that we recognize that there are basic rights that all people should enjoy. More and more, the laws of individual nation states, such as the United Kingdom, are being modified to fit into international human rights **legislation**. In 2000, the United Kingdom introduced a Human Rights Act for the first time.

Martin Luther King, the great campaigner for civil rights in the USA.

PART 3

THE LEGAL SYSTEM
Civil and criminal justice in Britain

There are many different laws, affecting every aspect of our lives. Broadly speaking we could divide the different kinds of law into two main categories: **civil law** and **criminal law**.

Civil law

Civil law (also known as private law) is about the relationships between individuals or companies and organizations. It is also about the relationship between individuals or companies and government departments (public law).

Civil law does not have **prosecutors** and **defendants**. Instead, it has a **plaintiff** or applicant (the person making a complaint) and a defendant or respondent (the person, or organization, or government department having to answer the complaint).

>> If you buy, for example, a videotape from a shop, you have entered into a **contract** with that shop: you have given them money in exchange for the tape. If the tape does not work, the shop has broken the contract. If the shop refuses to exchange it for a tape that works, you could make a civil claim against it under the law of contract.

>> If someone says something about you which is untrue and you are offended or in some way damaged by it (perhaps you are a shopkeeper and what has been said stops people using your shop), then they may be causing you a 'civil wrong' – the legal word is a **tort**.

>> If a married couple separate or wish to divorce, and cannot agree about who should care for their children, then they may use **family law** to help them.

>> Buying and selling houses or other property, and dividing up the property of people who have died is part of the law of property.

A procession of judges – a typical image of law for many people is that of old men wearing funny clothes, but there is much more to it than that.

Disputes between plaintiffs and defendants in any of these areas may go to court, but often an agreement is reached with the help of **solicitors** before anyone reaches a court. An agreement like this usually involves the payment of **damages** (money), but may also include a public apology being made. Sometimes injunctions are involved, which are **court orders** preventing the defendant from doing something again. In family law, an order may be drawn up that states what should happen to property or where children should live.

Criminal law

In civil law there is a dispute between individuals (or companies) who call in the legal experts and authorities to help them settle their differences. In criminal law, the dispute is with the state itself.

A crime is an act that is so serious and has such an effect on other people or society as a whole that the state steps in to deal with it.

Criminal wrongs are the subject of **prosecutions**. The police may catch a criminal and put together the evidence about his or her crime but in court, the **Crown Prosecution Service** (CPS), an independent agency, conducts the prosecution. Defendants (people accused of crimes) may use a solicitor or a **barrister** (the difference between the two is discussed on pages 28-29) to put their side of the case.

The CPS has to prove its case 'beyond a reasonable doubt'. This means that the **judge** or **jury** have to be no less than 'almost certain' that a crime has been committed and that the defendant did it.

If civil law is about enforcing a contract, compensating someone for a civil wrong, or deciding what should happen in the future, criminal law is about punishment – a fine or imprisonment, for example.

Sometimes criminal law and civil law is linked. If you steal a car, for example, you might be imprisoned for 'taking a motor vehicle without consent' (commonly known as a 'TWOC'), but you may also be made to pay compensation to the car owner for any damage you caused.

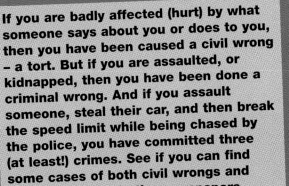

FIND OUT...

If you are badly affected (hurt) by what someone says about you or does to you, then you have been caused a civil wrong – a tort. But if you are assaulted, or kidnapped, then you have been done a criminal wrong. And if you assault someone, steal their car, and then break the speed limit while being chased by the police, you have committed three (at least!) crimes. See if you can find some cases of both civil wrongs and criminal wrongs in the newspapers.

THE LEGAL SYSTEM
The legal system in the United Kingdom

This diagram shows the different courts and processes that make up our legal system. Different courts deal with different types of disputes. Some of the most important parts of the legal system are explained over the next few pages.

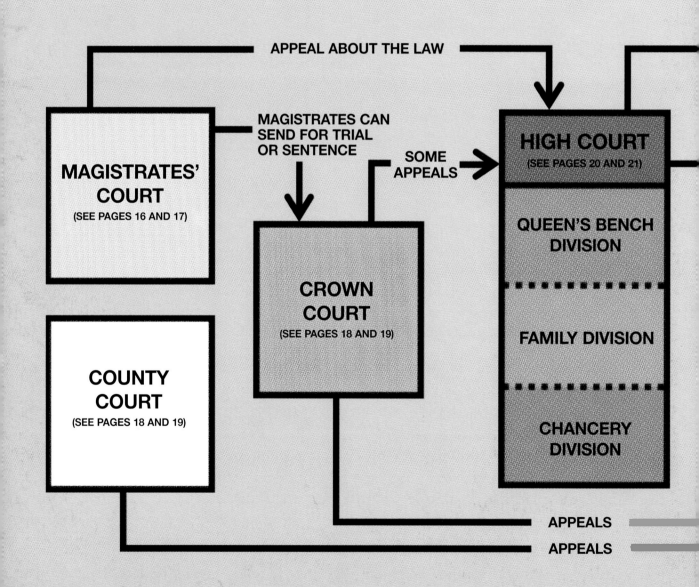

APPEAL ABOUT THE LAW

MAGISTRATES' COURT
(SEE PAGES 16 AND 17)

MAGISTRATES CAN SEND FOR TRIAL OR SENTENCE

SOME APPEALS

HIGH COURT
(SEE PAGES 20 AND 21)

QUEEN'S BENCH DIVISION

FAMILY DIVISION

CHANCERY DIVISION

CROWN COURT
(SEE PAGES 18 AND 19)

COUNTY COURT
(SEE PAGES 18 AND 19)

APPEALS

APPEALS

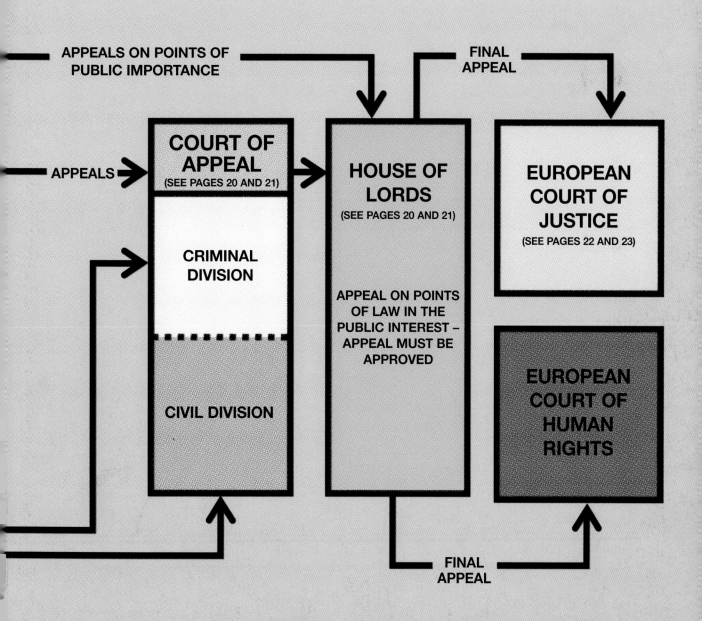

APPEALS ON POINTS OF
PUBLIC IMPORTANCE

FINAL
APPEAL

APPEALS

**COURT OF
APPEAL**
(SEE PAGES 20 AND 21)

**CRIMINAL
DIVISION**

CIVIL DIVISION

**HOUSE OF
LORDS**
(SEE PAGES 20 AND 21)

APPEAL ON POINTS
OF LAW IN THE
PUBLIC INTEREST –
APPEAL MUST BE
APPROVED

**EUROPEAN
COURT OF
JUSTICE**
(SEE PAGES 22 AND 23)

**EUROPEAN
COURT OF
HUMAN
RIGHTS**

FINAL
APPEAL

THE LEGAL SYSTEM
Magistrates in Britain

Magistrates are usually lay people (that is, not professionally trained **lawyers**) who are appointed to hear many criminal and **civil** cases. The official title of a magistrate is a 'Justice of the Peace', a name that goes back to the Justices of the Peace Act of 1341. This is a law that is still used today to make people keep the peace, or behave properly.

There are over 30,000 magistrates in England and Wales. They are not paid for their work, although they receive some compensation for loss of their earnings during the time they are 'sitting' (hearing cases in a magistrates' court). There is also a small number of stipendiary (paid, professional) magistrates.

Nearly all criminal cases, from traffic offences to murder, are first heard in magistrates' courts, and although the more serious ones go on to be heard by a judge and jury, more than 95 per cent are dealt with by magistrates.

This is a rather old fashioned Magistrates' courtroom, but the layout is very similar in the most modern courts.

Not everyone can be a magistrate. You have to be under 60 years old when appointed, and 'of good character' – you mustn't be bankrupt or have a criminal record. Members of the police force, traffic wardens, serving members of the armed forces, and Members of **Parliament** are among those who cannot serve because their work would conflict with that of the magistrates. Magistrates also have to be willing to have some basic training, and to serve for at least 26 sessions each year.

Some magistrates eventually specialize in **family courts** dealing with child protection or divorce cases, or youth courts, which deal with young offenders.

Magistrates usually sit as one of a group of two or three. A court clerk, who is more experienced in legal matters, helps them. The clerk is not supposed to tell magistrates what decision they should take, but he or she will give advice on points of law or procedure.

The Magistrates' Courts are a crucial part of the system of law and order in England and Wales. They deal with the vast majority of cases that come to court. They are not professional lawyers – your parents, or teachers or next-door neighbours could be magistrates. About half of Britain's magistrates are women. Five percent represent ethnic minorities. Although it is very unusual to be appointed as a magistrate under the age of thirty, there might be a lot to be gained if more 30 to 40 year olds took up the challenge.

Inside a magistrates' court

Although family courts are not open to the public because children are being discussed, it is possible to visit other magistrates' courts and watch what happens.

If you do, you will find that most cases are dealt with quite quickly. **Solicitors** will speak on behalf of clients, there may be witnesses, other court officials may comment, and the magistrates will probably go to their own room to think about what they have heard and come to a decision.

On a typical morning in a magistrates' court, the cases may be very varied. Motorists caught speeding will often plead guilty by letter. Someone picked up by the police the night before, lying drunk in the road, may be fined. Someone charged with a long list of offences of theft may be committed for trial in the **county court**. At the end of the morning, you might even see the chair of your Parent Teacher Association stand up. No, they're not on trial; they're just making an application for a licence to serve alcohol in the local church hall during a fund raising event for the school. Magistrates are responsible for giving licences to pubs and hotels as well.

THE LEGAL SYSTEM
The British Crown Court and county courts

Criminal cases that are either too serious or too complicated to be dealt with by **magistrates** will go to the **Crown Court** to be heard by a **judge** and **jury**. Civil cases which, for whatever reason cannot be heard by magistrates, go to the **county courts**.

The Crown Court

Although the Crown Court is perhaps the best-known court in England, it hears only about two per cent of criminal cases, the rest being dealt with by magistrates. Notice that we speak of 'the Crown Court': technically there is only one Crown Court. It was created by the Courts Act of 1971, and although it is divided between about 90 different centres in England and Wales, **lawyers** speak of it as a single thing.

The Crown Court is the place where you will see judges in their wigs and robes, **barristers** in gowns and wigs, and jury boxes and witness boxes. There is more formality than in a magistrates' court, but the public is allowed into a special area (the Public Gallery) to watch and listen.

Before the founding of the Crown Court, judges travelled from court to court in different towns and cities for 'the **assizes**'. A group of courts of this kind was called a circuit, and the name still remains for administrative purposes. Indeed, some of the judges who sit in the Crown Court are called 'circuit judges', while the more senior judges are called '**High Court**' judges. They deal with the most serious cases, such as murder and rape.

The most significant feature of the Crown Court is that it tries **defendants** by judge and jury. The judge listens to the case, sums up all the evidence for the jury and then asks them to go away to decide whether the defendant is guilty or not guilty. The jury must be convinced 'beyond reasonable doubt' before they can bring in a guilty **verdict**. When they have made their decision, it is up to the judge to pass **sentence** – to decide on the punishment.

The jury system is ancient. It was originally intended to ensure that a case against someone would be heard by those who knew him or her, that those with local knowledge could test the evidence and that the whole community would accept the final decision. Today members of the jury are unlikely to know anything about the person on trial, and are expected to take into account only what they hear in the court. The evidence may be complex or the case may depend upon scientific arguments. Certainly, juries are increasingly reliant upon the judge's summing up. Some people think that the time of the jury is over, and that cases should only be heard and decided by judges, with legal training and experience. What do you think?

The county courts

There are 270 county courts in England and Wales. They deal with civil cases – usually claims for money or the recovery of property. Over two million cases are started in the county courts every year, although many are settled 'out of court' (in 1995 there were less than 25,000 actual trials), and claims amounting to less than £1000 go to a special **'small claims' court**, where **plaintiffs** and defendants go before a judge in private for a decision to be made. This makes such cases both quicker and cheaper to decide. There are very rarely juries in the county courts: judges usually make decisions alone.

County courts also hear all divorce cases, although most divorces are granted by agreement between the man and woman and no one needs to attend court. There are only likely to be hearings if there is a dispute between the adults about the care of their children or the division of the family home, and then only if a special **'conciliation** service' has been unable to help.

FIND OUT...

Courts are expensive. There are many officials – judges, barristers and solicitors, clerks (administrators), police and Crown Prosecution Service – and cases which come to the Crown Court or a county court may last for days or even weeks. We live in a society where people increasingly want to go to court to settle their differences. This puts great pressure on the county courts in particular. A conciliation service for divorce matters and the small claims court has helped lessen the load – do you think there are other types of cases that could be dealt with outside court?

The Central Criminal Court ('Old Bailey') in the early nineteenth century. The prisoner is in 'the dock' on the right and the judge is sitting under the 'sword of justice' on the left. The jury are in the middle of the picture, the public in the gallery behind.

THE LEGAL SYSTEM
The British High Court and the House of Lords

County courts deal with most **civil law**, but the most complex civil cases, or those where a lot of money or property is involved, are heard by the **High Court**, usually in London. High Court **judges** work in three areas ('divisions') depending on what type of case they are dealing with.

High Court Family Division

This court deals with complex divorce cases but also, and most importantly, with the most difficult matters concerning the welfare of children. The Family Division judges also grant adoptions. Cases of this kind are usually heard in private – that is to say, the public is not admitted into the courtroom. Judges, **solicitors** and **barristers** who work in the Family Division are expected to have special skills in understanding the needs of children and families.

The Family Division also oversees arrangements for administering wills – how a person's property is divided up after his or her death. If no one objects to the proposals in a will, then the court will grant 'probate', allowing an 'executor' (often a solicitor, but it may be someone else – a family member or friend) to carry out the instructions in the will.

This is Dame Elizabeth Butler-Sloss, a famous High Court judge particularly concerned with the reform of family law.

High Court Chancery Division

When someone objects to the content of a will and probate cannot be granted, then the dispute goes to the **Chancery**. This division deals with the most complex cases about the division and ownership of property – not only wills, but also bankruptcy and disputes about the ownership of land.

The Chancery also deals with what is called 'intellectual property', which is a fast growing area for legal disputes. The words in this book are the subject of **copyright** – they belong to the person who published it. If someone else copies the book out and pretends it is their own work, they are infringing the publisher's copyright. Again, if you invent a computer game or a piece of computer software or a program, you may be able to claim that it is your intellectual property and that you must be paid for its use by anyone else.

The Queen's Bench Division of the High Court

The third part of the High Court deals with all other difficult civil cases, including debts, personal injury ('slander', when someone says something damaging and untrue about you, and 'libel', when the damaging and untrue fact is written down) or injuries caused by **negligence**.

The Appeal Court

The decision of any court can be taken to a higher court for appeal. The appeal might be against the conviction or the **sentence** (punishment), or because a mistake was made in how the law was interpreted. There can be appeals in criminal cases or in civil cases. Appeals against decisions in the High Court, county courts and the **Crown Court** go to the **Court of Appeal** in London. If lawyers are still not satisfied with the Court of Appeal's decision and wish to argue a point of law (not a point of fact), then they may be given leave (approval) by the Court of Appeal to have their case heard by the House of Lords. Members of a group of expert lawyers who are called Law Lords hear such appeals. Until recently, their decision was final, but now it is possible to take some cases either to the European Court of Justice or the European Court of Human Rights for further consideration.

Who's to blame?

If you are given the wrong medicine by a doctor or if you are badly hurt by a piece of metal falling from a crane when you are walking past a building site, you may be able to make a claim against an individual or a company. Was the doctor to blame? Or was it the person who wrongly labelled the medicine bottle? Or the hospital, for not training someone properly? Or, in the case of the crane, was there a notice warning passers-by of the dangers? Was it easily visible or had it been hidden? Or were you being careless in walking where you should not have? Who was responsible for the crane? The owner of the site? Or the owner of the crane?

To answer questions like these, many witnesses and a great deal of specialist knowledge may be required. Sometimes cases brought before the High Court can take a long time to be decided, and the issues might sometimes not seem very important. But the outcome of such cases can have a big impact and lead to changes in everyday life. New and clearer warning signs or changed training for people using equipment, improvements in working practices or in labelling – all of these might result from a finding of negligence in the High Court.

THE LEGAL SYSTEM
The European courts

Two years after the United Nations issued the Declaration of **Human Rights** in 1948, the Council of Europe, a group of European nations including the United Kingdom, drew up The European Convention on Human Rights and Fundamental Freedoms. The convention came into force in 1953, and is the key document used by the European Court of Human Rights, based in Strasbourg, in France.

In the time it has been in existence, the convention and the court have become more and more important. By 1997, over 40 states had signed up to the convention (including a number from eastern Europe). Although the original intention of the court was for a nation to bring a complaint against another nation, gradually individuals or groups have been allowed to make their own application to the court in Strasbourg. Cases usually concern the infringement of liberty. For instance, in 1971 the Republic of Ireland successfully argued that the government of the United Kingdom was behaving improperly in its treatment of people detained in Northern Ireland under "prevention of terrorism" **legislation**.

Other cases that have affected the United Kingdom have included the right of prisoners to write letters, and various cases involving **discrimination**. The European Court acts to uphold individual human **rights** and protect the **democratic** processes of government. All states, including the United Kingdom, are expected to change their own laws in line with the findings of the court in Strasbourg. This concerns some people who believe that it is no longer possible for British courts to make the final decision. Others argue that, as the United Kingdom is a part of Europe and has signed the convention, it is right that we should be bound by the findings of the Court of Human Rights.

European Court of Justice

This court has no direct connection with the European Court of Human Rights. The European Court of Justice is based in Luxembourg and was founded under the 1957 Treaty of Rome (which established the European Economic Community – since 1993 known as the European Union or EU). The EU has its own laws, created by treaties (binding agreements) that all member states must accept. The function of the European Court of Justice is to make sure that this happens. There are fifteen **judges** and nine advocates general (who advise the judges on the issues in particular cases), appointed from all the countries of the EU.

European law is wide-ranging and the judgements of the European Court of Justice have an impact in every country of the EU.

The European Court of Justice: one crucial difference from a British court is the number of judges present to hear a case and make a decision.

The European Community consists of fifteen member states with a total of 365 million **citizens**. Shared law is the basis of the community, and there is no doubt that European law will have the greatest impact on the development of law in the United Kingdom in the twenty-first century.

Key cases

In 1988, the European Court of Justice ruled that Denmark had a right to make distributors of beers and soft drinks set up deposit-and-return systems for empty bottles. In 1989, it ruled that a British tourist assaulted on the Paris Metro had a right to the same compensation as a French citizen. Perhaps most famous is the Bosman ruling of 1995, which allowed footballers greater freedom to be transferred between clubs, and also abolished the rule that there had to be a limit on the number of players from other EU countries in games between clubs – thus allowing many players of different nationalities to play for English clubs.

THE LEGAL SYSTEM
International law

International law is the law that deals with relations between nation states. With the growth of international trade and global organizations, international law is now also concerned with relations between these things and nation states, and in some cases between the states and individual people. International law may be found in bi-lateral (between two states) and multi-lateral (between many states) treaties – for example, agreements between two neighbouring states about the exact location of borders, or trade agreements between a number of states. International law has also developed in the judgements of the International Court of Justice and through various United Nations conventions. Here are some of the treaties and conventions of the past 60 years that show how varied and important international law is:

>> The Charter of the United Nations and the Statute of the International Court of Justice (1945)

>> The Universal Declaration on Human Rights (1948)

>> UN Convention on the Law of the Sea (1982)

>> Convention on International Trade in Endangered Species (1973)

>> International Convention for the Suppression of Terrorist Bombings (1997)

>> Comprehensive Nuclear Test Ban Treaty (1996).

The International Court of Justice

Like all laws, international laws work best by agreement, but from time to time need to be enforced. The United Nations has this role. At times the UN also has to take on a peacekeeping role, as in the former Yugoslavia during the 1990s. If the UN acts as something like an international police force, the International Court of Justice, based at The Hague in the Netherlands is its court. This court consists of fifteen **judges**, appointed for nine-year terms, who hear disputes between states. These disputes again vary widely. In 2001, for example, the court was dealing with more than twenty cases, including a dispute between Iran and the USA about oil platforms, boundary disputes between Cameroon and Nigeria and between Nicaragua and Honduras, as well as a dispute on the 'legality of the use of force' between Yugoslavia and the nations involved in the United Nations Peacekeeping Forces in the Balkans.

The International Criminal Court

International law has also been used to try individuals for war crimes. The Nuremberg Trials following the Second World War began this process. In 1994, the International Criminal Court was established, also at The Hague. Today, there are **tribunals** at the International Criminal Court that look at war crimes and claims of ethnic cleansing and genocide in the former Yugoslav states, as well as in Rwanda in Africa.

For many years there has been co-operation between the police forces of nation states, and **extradition** treaties between many states, which prevent people wanted for crime in one country from simply moving to another. As Kofi Annan, the Secretary-General of the United Nations said in 1994:

❝In the prospect of an international criminal court lies the promise of universal justice. That is the simple and soaring hope of this vision. We are close to its realization. We will do our part to see it through till the end. We ask you... to do yours in our struggle to ensure that no ruler, no state, no junta and no army anywhere can abuse human rights with impunity. Only then will the innocents of distant wars and conflicts know that they, too, may sleep under the cover of justice; that they, too, have rights, and that those who violate those rights will be punished.❞

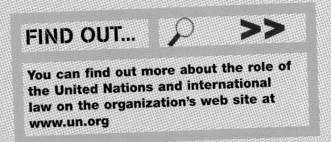

FIND OUT...

You can find out more about the role of the United Nations and international law on the organization's web site at www.un.org

The Nuremberg trials after the Second World War tried individual members of the German Nazi party for crimes committed during the war. The defendants are sitting in two rows in front of the line of military policemen.

THE LAW IN ACTION
Systems of law

How do we settle disputes? We might fight it out to see who wins – though that won't tell us what the truth was, only which person was the strongest. We might negotiate – a more refined kind of fight in which words and the powers of persuasion replace sticks, knives or guns. But this, too, will only tell us who has the best argument (or who can be most persuasive), and not necessarily what the truth is. We might ask an independent person to look at every side of the disagreement and keep looking until the truth emerges, though this might take a very long time. Systems of law move between these three different ways of settling disputes, although the system in the United Kingdom is a combination of the first two, and is often known as the 'adversarial system'. The approach in many other countries, including our European neighbours, favours the third, often called the 'inquisitorial system'.

Is a trial about winning an argument or about finding out the truth? Some people think that these two things can be the same and that, as long as there are rules, and people stick to them, then the adversarial system does allow the truth to come out. Other people point to some problems: the adversarial system assumes **equality** between the sides.

Two knights in combat to the death – this is an illustration from a medieval manuscript.

The adversarial system

Imagine two medieval knights in combat. They fight until one is exhausted, and the loser is killed (or allowed to live, defeated and ashamed). Some people feel the justice system in the United Kingdom is like that. In essence, it sets two people against each other: a **prosecutor** and an accused, or a **plaintiff** and a **defendant** (in **civil law**), letting them fight it out with words, with the help of people skilled in argument, calling witnesses to back up their arguments, and doing all they can to trip up their opponent. The name of the game is winning.

A judge in such a battle is bit like a referee, trying to ensure fair play, within the well-established rules, but never interfering. Imagine a referee in a football match who decided that one side would be better if a player was substituted, or who headed the ball into the net when he got the chance. We would think that would not bring about a fair result.

The statue of **Justice** on top of the **Old Bailey** holds a pair of weighing scales in her hand. This suggests that both sides have an equal chance, and only truth will tip the scales one way or the other. Unfortunately, there are other ways of tipping the scales: there may not have been time to gather all the evidence (or some evidence may have been withheld, or interpreted wrongly). One side may have a better advocate (the person speaking on their behalf – often a **barrister**) than the other.

Finally, the adversarial system depends entirely on what is presented to the court – to the **judge** and **jury**. They have to make their decisions based only on this. As Lord Denning (a famous British judge) once said, 'the judge is not allowed…to call a witness whom he thinks might throw some light on the facts. He must rest content with the witnesses called by the parties.'

The inquisitorial system

Judges in the inquisitorial system are not only *allowed* to make their own investigations, it is what they *must* do. Unlike judges in the United Kingdom, judges in France or Germany, for instance, must actively seek out evidence and information, call any witness and make any investigation necessary to find out the truth – what actually happened, or what was promised, or whatever the matter in dispute might be.

Many people think that this seems so obviously a better way than the adversarial system, that they cannot understand why it is not the norm. But opponents of the inquisitorial system point out that this search for truth can take a long time and be expensive so, that in practice, judges tend to stop their investigations when they are near enough to the truth for everyone to feel satisfied.

In fact, modern systems of law borrow from each other. In the United Kingdom, judges, although still firmly committed to the adversarial system, make their own limited investigations, for example in **family law** (trying to discover the wishes and needs of children in care cases, for instance). They may try to negotiate agreements in small claims cases or disputes between parties in civil cases.

THE LAW IN ACTION
Solicitors, barristers and judges

The legal profession covers a range of people – from **High Court Judges** to secretaries in **solicitors**' practices or **barristers**' chambers. The legal profession operates at many different levels of skill. There is a wide range of income – a 'star' barrister may be paid thousands of pounds for a day in court, while a secretary in a local authority's legal department will probably not get much more than that for a whole year's work.

Everyone involved in the legal process shares a great deal: specialist knowledge and skill, a common language which may seem strange to an outsider (**lawyers** talk about 'briefs', 'litigation' or use Latin phrases such as *'ratio decidendi'* – the process of reasoning that leads to a decision), and particular places: courtrooms, barristers' chambers, solicitors' offices.

Although many different people are involved in bringing a legal case to court, and arguing the case, three professional groups are particularly important: solicitors, barristers and judges.

Solicitors

A solicitor gives specialist legal help and advice. There are over 60,000 solicitors in England and Wales and they work in many different settings. Some are employed by local authorities to advise on planning applications (can Mr Smith build a house in that place?), on education or social services matters, or on employment. Others work for large industries or in commerce. Some are employed by the **Crown Prosecution Service**, and help to decide which cases should be taken to court.

Most solicitors work in private practice, usually in partnership with others. Much of this private work is about conveyancing (helping people buy and sell their houses) or helping people make their wills. Other solicitors specialize in family work (divorce, adoption, child protection) and some work only in **criminal law**. Solicitors prepare cases to be heard in court and may speak on behalf of their clients in **magistrates** and **county courts** (and very occasionally in the **Crown Court**).

Barristers

Barristers are also specialist legal advisers who have particular skills in arguing cases in court. They are trained and skilled in presenting cases in court, but are also able to advise solicitors and clients on whether or not a case can be won.

There are about 8,000 practising barristers in England and Wales who work independently of solicitors and of each other, though they often share offices (called chambers) and may share staff, too. Another 2500 barristers are employed by local authorities, or work in industry and commerce for example, wherever their specialist skills are needed.

It is the image of the barrister in wig and gown, skilfully cross-examining a witness to reveal the truth that represents the law for many people. Barristers' court work is mainly in the Crown Court, the High Court or the appeal courts. Very skilled senior barristers become **Queen's Counsel** (QC) and will take on the most complex cases of all. Many judges have first become QCs (the lawyer's phrase is 'take silk').

Judges

The job of the judge is to make sure that court cases are conducted fairly, according to the law, and to rule on points of law – that is, to decide what the law says and what it means. In county courts and the High Court, the judge will decide the outcome of the case having heard the arguments. In the Crown Court, a **jury** decides whether a **defendant** is innocent or guilty, and the judge's job is to summarize the evidence the jury has heard and tell the jury members how the law needs to be applied before they go away to make their decision. If the jury returns a guilty **verdict**, then the judge will **sentence** the convicted person (decide on the punishment).

George Carman QC, one of the most famous barristers of the late twentieth century.

FIND OUT...

There is often criticism that the legal profession does not come from a wide enough cross-section of society. This is probably not true of solicitors, but many people are concerned that not enough women or members of ethnic minority groups become barristers and judges. Although solicitors and barristers are trained, judges have only recently begun to have any sort of training. They are often criticized for seeming remote from the ordinary people who are involved in the case. Some people think that judges need to be more skilled in explaining the law and helping people in court understand what is happening to them. Why not find a time to go to a Crown Court? Watch and listen – what do you think about the judges and barristers at work there?

THE LAW IN ACTION
The police, law and order

A brief history

Before the Norman Conquest of 1066, the first police constables, known as tything-men, were elected representatives of their community, responsible to a Shire-Reeve or Sheriff for making sure that laws were upheld and peace maintained in their community. In the Middle Ages, the tything-man became the 'parish constable' and the Shire-Reeve became a Justice of the Peace, himself responsible to the High Sheriff of the county.

This system was well suited to small rural communities, but with the growth of towns and cities in the eighteenth century, the system began to fall apart. By the early nineteenth century, the need for a different system had become urgent and, in 1829, the Metropolitan Police was founded for the London area (not including the City of London).

The role of a police force

The first Commissioner of the Metropolitan Police, Sir Richard Mayne, defined the task of a police force in 1829, and his words still summarize the role of the police today:

"The primary object of an efficient police is the prevention of crime; the next, that of detection and punishment of offenders if crime is committed. To these ends all the efforts of police must be directed. The protection of life and property, the preservation of public tranquillity, and the absence of crime, will alone prove whether those efforts have been successful and whether the objects for which the police were appointed have been attained."

However, the police can be used not only to protect life and property and to preserve public tranquillity ('law' and 'order'), but also to control people according to the will of a ruler. We speak of police states where the police repress and control communities, as in South Africa during the apartheid regime, or the role of the SS in Nazi Germany. Sometimes people think that police forces have been drawn into repression and become the instruments of a dominant group, no longer behaving fairly to the whole community. Some people have said that the way the police were used during the miners' strike in 1983 was also inappropriate.

Certainly in a modern, **multi-cultural** and complex society, it is not easy for the police both to be and to appear to be acting fairly towards everyone. A recent example might help us to think about this problem.

Stephen Lawrence

On 22 April 1993, two young black men, Stephen Lawrence and Duwayne Brooks, were attacked in south-east London by a group of youths. Stephen died from stab wounds. The police investigated the killing, but were heavily criticized by Stephen's parents and others for their actions. The police did not treat the attack as racially motivated and were increasingly seen by the black community as full of 'racist prejudice, stereotyping and insensitivity', while the investigating team showed 'inappropriate behaviour and patronizing attitudes' to the dead man's family. After many investigations into the circumstances of Stephen's death and of the police investigation, a public inquiry was held which concluded that the Metropolitan police was 'institutionally racist', and that these attitudes had led to a failure to make a proper investigation of Stephen's killing.

The Stephen Lawrence Inquiry defined institutional racism as:

❝The collective failure of an organization to provide an appropriate and professional service to people because of their colour, culture or ethnic origin. It can be seen or detected in processes, attitudes and behaviour which amount to discrimination through unwitting prejudice, ignorance, thoughtlessness and racist stereotyping which disadvantage minority ethnic people.❞

Since the Lawrence enquiry, police forces throughout the country have begun to work to overcome this sense of institutional racism, increasing efforts to recruit officers from all sections of the community.

THE LAW IN ACTION
Being punished

We assume that someone who has done wrong and has been found out will be punished. We also assume that the punishment will be just – that it will be fair and fitting. But there are many questions hidden behind these assumptions. What is **justice**? What is punishment for? What do we think we are doing when we punish somebody?

Justice

We can talk about justice in a narrow sense or a wide sense. In a wide sense, we may talk about a 'just society', and mean by that, perhaps, a society in which people are treated fairly and equally, where their **rights** are respected and where they can be safe. In the narrower sense, we might say that justice means making sure that laws are obeyed, and that people who break laws are punished. We might also want to say that a just society in the wider sense will have just laws. But a just society in the narrower sense – where the rule of law is upheld – may not be a just society in the wider sense – South Africa under apartheid is an example, where laws were unfair on the majority of the population.

Punishment

What we think justice is will affect our attitude to punishment. But it is important to see that for most people, a just society is one in which the legal system not only decides whether an offence has been committed, but also sets the level of punishment and administers it.

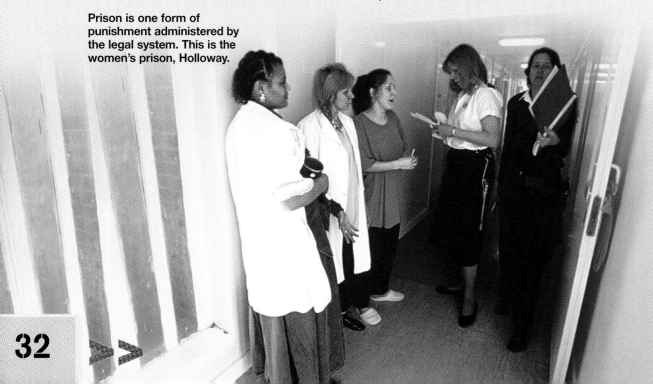

Prison is one form of punishment administered by the legal system. This is the women's prison, Holloway.

Assuming, as most people do, that wrongdoing should be punished, there are essentially two approaches that might be taken: one looking 'backwards', the other looking 'forwards':

>> Retribution. Some people argue that wrongdoing must always be punished, and that the punishment should always 'fit the crime' – the more serious the offence, the greater the penalty to be paid. This argument concentrates on the past: an offence has been committed and no other factors are relevant. There is a simple and straightforward connection between crime and punishment; nothing else will satisfy the demands of justice and fairness.

>> Consider the consequences. Other people argue that when someone does wrong, the most important factor is not what happened in the past, but the consequences for the future. Using this argument, the purpose of punishment is closely linked to the effects it will have. Someone may be punished in order to protect society (so that a serial killer, serial rapist or habitual burglar will be sent to prison so that that person cannot continue their offending). Or a court may be deliberately lenient – a fine, or community service, rather than prison, say – in the hope that there will be no further offending behaviour. Therefore, a major factor in deciding how to punish an offence will be how the offender can be helped not to offend again. This aim of **rehabilitation** is very important in modern theories of punishment.

There are very strong disagreements between those who hold these two opposing theories of punishment.

Capital punishment

Capital punishment is the practice of the state-approved (and administered) taking of life as punishment for a crime. In the past, many offences were 'capital crimes'. The death penalty has been abolished in the United Kingdom and Europe for many years, but is still allowed in some countries – in certain states of America, for example.

The only arguments for the death penalty come from the retribution view of punishment: that the death penalty acts either as state-sponsored revenge on behalf of the victim and their family, or as a **deterrent**. Unfortunately, the high murder rate in America suggests that it hardly acts as a deterrent, and some argue that its presence in any society is little more than a mirror of the violence that society creates and accepts.

The opponents of capital punishment argue that nothing can justify the taking of a life. They argue that, while nothing can ever excuse murder, the right to life is of primary importance, and not even committing a murder should mean that someone else's life can be taken away. The true function of punishment, they would argue, is to prevent crime and rehabilitate criminals, by helping offenders face the consequences of their actions. What do you think?

THE LAW AND YOU
Children, young people and the law

In 1989, the United Nations adopted a Convention on the Rights of the Child. This set out a picture of the sort of lives children and young people needed to have in order to be protected from harm and to be brought up to live 'in the spirit of peace, dignity, tolerance, freedom, **equality** and solidarity' – in other words, to take their place as fully adult members of society.

The government of the United Kingdom accepted this convention, and its aims entered British law as the Children Act, 1989. The Children Act sets out to balance two key principles. First, (and most importantly) is that in all questions about the upbringing of children, 'the child's welfare shall be… the paramount [most important] consideration.'

Secondly, the Children Act recognizes that it is best for children to be brought up within their families, and that parents should be responsible for the welfare of their children. However, it also accepts that sometimes parents are unwilling or unable to meet the needs of their children, in which case the state will step in to help.

The Children Act understands that children and young people have a right to develop physically, mentally, and morally; they have a right to education, and they have a right to be protected from abuse, whether physical, emotional or sexual. A child or young person's right to family life means that they should know who is going to care for them. Ideally, this should be their own natural family, but sometimes they may need to live away from home – for a short time, or sometimes for many years. They may even stop having any contact with their birth family and be adopted by another family.

Since 1989, the court system has developed to try to recognize the stress children and young people can be under when they experience family difficulties. **Family courts** are quite separate from other courts, although cases may be heard by **magistrates**, **judges** or **High Court** judges, depending on the difficulty of the issues involved. **Solicitors** and **barristers** working with children will often make a positive decision to do so – it will rarely be 'just another job' – and will have special skills in talking to children and young people and understanding their needs.

Courts also appoint special workers to work closely with children and young people and advise judges and magistrates on what is best. Although **social workers** and parents will have their own views, the courts recognize that the child's voice can often be drowned out by arguments between the adults, and do all they can to prevent this from happening.

These **probation officers** have had special training to develop the skills which they can use to help and work with young offenders.

When parents decide to separate or divorce, children can often find themselves in difficulties, unsure about where they will live and how they will keep in contact with the parent they are not living with. **County courts** and, sometimes, magistrates' courts, can be involved in helping with these decisions, too. Again, they must make sure that the welfare of the child is paramount – which doesn't always mean doing what a child wants; it means trying to do what is best for a child. Parents are encouraged to go to the **Conciliation Service** to discuss the situation and try to come to an agreement, and children's views will always be asked for, too.

FIND OUT...

In Bertolt Brecht's play *The Caucasian Chalk Circle*, there is a famous scene where a judge is asked to decide who has most right to keep a child – a natural mother or the woman who has cared for him and kept him alive. The case is difficult because both women seem to have a strong claim. Try to find a copy of the play and read, or better still act out, how the judge, Azdak, makes his decision. Is he right? But one thing is clear: whatever he decides, someone will be unhappy. This is the great difficulty of so many court cases in family law. They involve a lot of pain and distress, and they are some of the most difficult cases for lawyers as well as for the families involved.

THE LAW AND YOU
Young offenders

In England and Wales, no one under the age of ten can be charged with a criminal offence or appear in a criminal court. Young offenders are people between the age of ten and eighteen who are charged with committing a crime. Because young offenders are under the age of eighteen, they are also subject to the protection of the Children Act 1989, which states that their welfare must be the first consideration in anything that happens.

What happens if I am arrested?

This young prisoner in California is learning a trade whilst in custody.

>> The police can only interview you if either one of your parents or some other 'appropriate adult' (usually a **social worker**) is with you. You, or the adult with you, can also ask for a **solicitor** to be present as well.

>> You can only be held for a maximum of 24 hours without being taken to court for an extension, which can only be granted for periods of 12 hours at a time. After questioning you, the police may decide that you are innocent, or that the offence was minor and they will take no further action. They might formally caution you – a senior police officer will warn you about your future behaviour.

>> If the offence is serious, the police may decide that you should go to a youth court, where **magistrates** skilled in dealing with young people will decide whether you should be allowed home on **bail**, or be **remanded**, either to the care of the local authority, (you may be taken to a foster home or a children's home) or, if people think you may run away and put yourself or other people at risk, you may be sent to a secure unit.

Bail and remand

With bail, there may be conditions attached about whom you can see and where you can go. You will also be given a time to report to the police and to return to court. Not doing any of these things is a serious offence (often more serious than the offence you may have been charged with) and will be treated seriously by the courts and the police.

If you are remanded to the care of the local authority, to a home or a secure unit, your welfare and situation will be kept under constant review.

Periods of bail or remand may last a long time. The police and **Crown Prosecution Service** have to prepare the case against you, and your own solicitor has to prepare your defence (if you are pleading not guilty) or arguments on your behalf (if you are admitting the offence).

A **probation officer** or social worker from the local authority's Young Offenders' Team (YOT) will usually also prepare a report about you and about the offence.

What will happen if I'm found guilty?

There are several possible outcomes (usually called disposals):

>> You may be discharged – either an absolute discharge, in which the court decides to take no further action, or a conditional discharge which means that nothing is done now, but if you return to court (usually within a year) you will be resentenced for this offence.

>> You (or sometimes your parents) may be fined.

>> You may be required to spend time at an attendance centre for two hours, twice a month. A **sentence** will usually demand between six and eighteen separate attendances.

>> You may be given a supervision order or probation order. These usually last for one year, but may be for up to three. You will have to keep in touch with a social worker or probation officer from the YOT whose duty is to 'advise, assist and befriend' you.

>> You may receive a community service order for up to 240 hours (100 hours is more usual). You will be expected to spend up to eight hours under supervision each week doing useful tasks in the community.

>> As well as passing one of these sentences, a court may 'bind-over' your parent(s) to take proper control of you and make sure you comply with the sentence you have been given. You may also be put on a curfew order or even be monitored electronically to reduce the risk of reoffending.

>> Most seriously, you may be given custody. Young people convicted of murder or **manslaughter** will go to a secure unit (a children's home with locked doors) until they are old enough to be released or go on to a Young Offender Institution (YOI).

THE LAW AND YOU
Justice in a multi-cultural society

The current legal system in the United Kingdom began to be created shortly after the Norman Conquest in the eleventh century, although some elements date back to Anglo-Saxon times. It has developed as an adversarial system of law (see pages 26–27), in which two people, usually referred to as 'parties' (a **prosecutor** and accused in **criminal law**, or a **plaintiff** and **defendant** in **civil law**) argue their case, with the help of experts, in front of **magistrates**, a **judge** and, sometimes, a **jury**. The laws of the United Kingdom have developed over centuries just as British society has developed, and have changed as the needs of that society have changed.

For instance, as England became an important trading nation, so many more laws were created to govern trade, and to ensure that **contracts** were kept. Later, as the British Empire grew, the legal system was taken over to the countries that were now under British rule. The new British rulers of those countries liked to talk about how they had brought law and order with them, but in fact they were simply replacing one system of law by another, just as William the Conqueror and his French army had brought a new law to Britain to replace that of the defeated Saxons.

The police in Britain are actively encouraging people from a wide spread of cultures to join the force. They hope to reach a point where all cultures are represented fairly amongst the ranks.

Today, the United Kingdom is a complex **multi-cultural** society. Many people are concerned that the law has not been able to keep up with this, and some people think that the current system of policing is actually preventing good relations between cultures.

Research has shown that there is a strong belief that young black man are more likely to commit crimes than other groups of people. This belief may be reinforced whenever a young black man is found to have actually committed a crime. It is reinforced even further when closed circuit television cameras follow young black men and catch them in criminal activity. However, the belief is quite wrong. All ages, from all cultural groups and both sexes may commit crimes. In any case, 95 per cent of the population is white, so there must be more white criminals than non-white criminals.

Unfortunately, the racist belief remains and it can create not just individual prejudice, but also what has been called institutional racism. Institutional racism has been defined as:

❝The collective failure of an organization to provide appropriate and professional service to people because of their colour, culture or ethnic origins. It can be seen… in processes, attitudes and behaviour which amount to discrimination through unwitting prejudice, ignorance, thoughtlessness and racial stereotyping.❞

This was how the investigation into the death of Stephen Lawrence defined the attitude of the Metropolitan Police when they failed to recognize his murder as having been racially motivated.

Laws such as the Race Relations Act have tried to stamp out racist behaviour, but many people believe that institutional racism still dominates much of British society, and that even the legal system is unable to escape some of this criticism. Do you think this is fair?

Members of ethnic minority groups are not very well represented within the police, or among **solicitors**, **barristers** or judges. Do you think this makes a difference to how decisions are made?

The development of European law has undoubtedly modified the legal practices, and actual laws, of the United Kingdom over the past thirty or so years. Could you imagine this developing further?

FIND OUT...

Another aspect of law in a multi-cultural society is the extent to which a legal system can take into account the beliefs, practices and laws of other cultures. In your opinion, how far should the United Kingdom law take into account the legal practices of Islam, for example? Do you think that there will come a time when current laws will be modified to take account of the range of beliefs and practices of our multi-cultural society?

THE LAW AND YOU
The future

The United Kingdom's legal system is constantly changing. This is partly the effect of **case law**, which is the way in which decisions made by a **judge** about a particular case may be seen as creating a **precedent** for the way in which a similar case is dealt with in the future. Or it may be the effect of **legislation** – either 'primary legislation' (Acts of Parliament – for example, the Children Act, 1989) or 'secondary legislation', in which government ministers issue 'guidance' to add greater detail to the Act (the Children Act has eight volumes of detailed guidance covering everything from childminders to the arrangements for children leaving care).

Case law versus legislation

The debate about the relative advantages of case law and legislation is likely to become increasingly important. The great strength of case law is the way it has been formed by judges listening to real arguments about real disputes or **alleged** crimes. The main weakness of case law, however, is its complexity. Understanding what has been decided in the past is no easy matter, and judges, **barristers** and **solicitors** need to be skilled in interpreting what a judge might have meant when he made a decision (often expressed in complex legal language), and also how far it applies to the case they are now thinking about.

Legislation may also have its difficulties. Laws made by **Parliament** will often be the result of political attitudes. For example, a political party with racist beliefs might make laws to limit **immigration** or even remove groups of people from the country – just as the Nazi party in Germany in the 1930s passed laws against Jewish people.

Secondary legislation (guidance) is never debated by Parliament. While it often outlines the best professional practice of the day – for example in the care of children or in race relations – it might also enable government ministers to slip in unpopular or questionable practices which then, without debate, have the force of law.

All of this contrasts strongly with legal systems that depend upon a code of law – a set of written laws. Such law codes date back nearly 4000 years.The advantages of law codes are that they are 'internally coherent' – they are the result of a careful set of decisions made at one time – and that they are comparatively simple to use. The disadvantage is that they may easily become out-dated and create major problems when societies change.

The European dimension

The development of the European Union, built upon a shared set of laws, means that the 'legislation-plus-case-law' model of UK law will have to find ways of co-existing with the much more code-based models that exist in other European countries. This has already begun to happen in the development of **human rights** legislation, a European initiative brought into the UK legal system, and likely to radically modify other UK legislation.

The rights of the citizen

A second crucial debate in the future is likely to focus on the idea of 'citizenship'. Many countries have, as the basis of their legal system, a Bill of **Rights** that sets out the rights of a **citizen** of that country. The United Kingdom does not have such a bill, although many people argue that the Human Rights Act, 1998, is the first step towards one. Traditionally, United Kingdom legislation has been dominated by the desire to protect people from one another and to help them sort out their disputes. But a Bill of Rights turns the whole thing round. The essential idea is one of **equality** and freedom: as the United States Declaration puts it, we are all 'created equal… and endowed with certain rights…' Central to the debate about citizenship is whether the United Kingdom should move towards a culture focused on human rights.

Finally, we may see how the law needs to take on board the challenges of a **multi-cultural** society. Not only will it be important to make sure that people of many different cultural backgrounds work in the legal professions and the police, but there will also be the need to make sure that the laws themselves reflect the wishes and needs, and the religious and cultural backgrounds of a range of community groups.

Behind these challenges there is a fundamental question: how can law and order in the twenty-first century help guarantee freedom, democracy and human rights in a multi-cultural society?

DEBATE
Debating the issues

The law is a complex subject. Although the most exciting and colourful elements are undoubtedly to be found in criminal cases in the **Crown Court**, with **judges** and **barristers** in wigs and gowns, **juries**, the cross-examination of witnesses, and the drama of discovering what the **verdict** of the court will be, this is only a tiny part of the whole legal picture. The processes of law can range from the granting of a licence to serve alcohol at a PTA event, through claims for compensation following an accident, right across to international trade or land disputes.

In this book, we have only been able to touch on a few elements of law and order.

But nevertheless, each one of these can be a good subject for further exploration. So why not put the law itself on trial?

FIND OUT...

You can observe the adversarial system in operation in any magistrates' court, and especially in the Crown Court. The inquisitorial system is a much more European model, but there is a good summary of how it works on the European Court of Justice's web site. Have a look at it: www.europa.eu.int/cj

The scales of Justice are meant to represent weighing the evidence, fairly and impartially.

Which system of law is most effective?

We have asked a lot of questions in the book – and you will no doubt have many more. One particular question was about how law gets at the truth. We said that there were two basic systems of law: the adversarial system and the inquisitorial system. We suggested that both had strengths and weaknesses. You might like to put that to the test, too.

Why not take a subject or question about the way the law works (or doesn't work!) that you feel strongly about, and argue it out using both the adversarial and the inquisitorial system? You might want to ask whether the law is institutionally racist, or whether it can properly protect children. You might want to ask why there are so few women judges. You might even take an actual recent court case, or a historical event that you've been studying or can easily find out plenty about, and set up your own trial.

>> For the adversarial system you would need a **plaintiff** and a **defendant**, or a **prosecutor** and an accused if you decide it's a criminal trial. You would also need people good at arguing the case, witnesses for both sides, a jury and a judge. Remember that the judge is only a referee – but will need to be able to sum up the arguments on both sides before the jury makes a decision.

>> For the inquisitorial system, you would need someone to make a complaint and someone to answer it. You would also need a panel of judges who would have the power to ask for any evidence they think might be necessary to answer the question, and plenty of people prepared to go off and research the answers before coming back as witnesses. You might have to be prepared to take a long time over this sort of trial!

FIND OUT...

The policy of sentencing young people has changed greatly in the past 20 years, with a move away from punishment in custody towards help in the community. Although the policy of keeping young people out of prison seems to have successfully reduced the numbers of young people committing crimes, some critics have said that this is too lenient and is leading to an attitude that crime doesn't matter.
What do you think?

FURTHER RESOURCES

The law is a very complex subject and is always changing. A very good website giving an overview of many aspects of law is UK Law Online which can be found at:
www.leeds.ac.uk/law/hamlyn

You can find out more about solicitors at:
www.lawsociety.org.uk

Information about the prison service can be found at:
www.homeoffice.gov.uk/hmipris/hmipris.htm

One of the leading organizations concerned about prisons and the treatment of prisoners is the Howard League for Penal Reform:
web.ukonline.co.uk/howard.league/

The law as it relates to young people accused or convicted of offences has been changing recently. There is good information on these developments at the sites of the Youth Justice Board:
www.youth-justice-board.gov.uk
and the National Association for Youth Justice at:
www.nayj.org.uk

Many police forces in the UK have their own websites, which you can easily find through a search engine. One of the most informative sites is that of the Metropolitan Police (responsible for policing most of London). The address is:
www.met.police.uk

Many questions and criticisms about the law, and especially how it is used, are asked by groups concerned with civil and human rights. One of the most important of these in the United Kingdom is the National Council for Civil Liberties/Liberty.
Their address is:
21 Tabard Street, London SE1 4LA

Their website is
www.liberty-human-rights.org.uk

What are the rights and responsibilities of being a citizen? There are some good websites with lots of good ideas and information for young people at The Citizenship Foundation:
www.citfou.org.uk
and The Institute for Citizenship
www.citizen.org.uk

The Home Office (that part of the UK government responsible for law and order) has a Human Rights Task Force. Their website is:
www.humanrights.gov.uk

Law in the United Kingdom is becoming increasingly closely linked to the legal systems of Europe. For more information about the European Court of Human Rights you can visit:
www.echr.coe.int
and information about the European Court of Justice can be found at:
http://europa.eu.int/cj/en/index.htm

Finally, don't forget to visit the web pages of the United Nations Association for information about law and justice throughout the world:
www.un.org

Films and television programmes about the police and the law are always exciting and give some useful information. But a very good resource can be found in your nearest town or city. Anyone can visit Magistrates' Courts and Crown Courts to watch and listen to the law in action: they might be less exciting than television soap or a film, but they are the real thing!

Two great plays include trials that could be re-enacted by groups:

Aeschylus' ancient Greek play 'The Eumenides' (The Kindly Ones) is the last part of the trilogy of revenge called *Oresteia*. The play is nearly 2500 years old: the issues it raises are very modern.

Bertolt Brecht's play 'The Caucasian Chalk Circle' was written more recently, just over 50 years ago. Find the trial presided over by Judge Azdak – would you have done the same?

GLOSSARY

alleged — to assert something to be true. Whether it is true or not has still to be proved.

assizes — before 1972, the criminal courts in different towns of England and Wales that were visited by a travelling judge to hear cases

bail — when a person accused of a crime is allowed limited freedom until the case is decided

barrister — someone qualified to argue a case before a judge (and jury)

capital punishment — a decision by the state that someone should be put to death as a punishment for a crime they have committed

case law — laws that have been created by decisions made by judges in earlier cases

Chancery — the court dealing with the most complex cases concerning money and property

citizen — a person with certain freedoms guaranteed by the state in which they live

civil law — That part of the law concerning disputes between individuals, companies, organizations and government departments

conciliation — attempts to help people agree their differences outside the courtroom

contract — an agreement between two parties (individuals, organizations etc). Much of civil law is concerned with alleged failures to keep contracts.

copyright — the right to reproduce (copy) anything

county court — the courts in which judges hear civil law cases

Court of Appeal — a court where disagreements about the correctness of legal decisions are heard

court order — in civil law – an order made by a court preventing someone from doing something (for example an order preventing a violent man from coming near his wife and children)

criminal law — that part of the law dealing with serious matters (crimes) such as theft, murder or rape

Crown Court — the court where criminal cases are heard

Crown Prosecution Service — the organization that decides whether someone should be tried for a criminal offence, and then conducts that prosecution in court

damages — anything (usually money) paid to compensate someone under civil law

defendant — someone accused of a crime

democratic — from two Greek words meaning 'rule by the people' – a political system aiming to bring about equal rights for everyone

deterrent — a punishment given to put others off from committing similar offences

discrimination — treating an individual or a group differently because of their race, gender, sexual orientation or physical disabilities, for instance

equality — treating everyone in exactly the same way, offering everyone the same opportunities

extradition — an agreement between states to send someone alleged to have committed a crime back to their own country for trial

family court — a place where decisions about disputes in family life and about children can be dealt with

family law — that part of the law dealing with families and children

High Court — where senior judges make decisions in the most complex cases

human rights — the belief that there are some things that are necessary to enable people to live a properly human existence

immigration — moving permanently to live in one country from another one

indigenous — people who were born and whose families have lived in a place for a long time

inequality — the opposite of equality, where people are treated differently and not given the same opportunities

judges	senior lawyers who oversee cases in County Courts, the Crown Court and the High Court
jury	a group of (usually 12) men and women selected at random to listen to arguments in a court and to decide whether an accused person is guilty of an alleged offence
justice	an attempt to judge impartially and fairly ('without fear or favour') between two parties in a dispute: and – ensuring that wrongdoing is punished: and – creating a society based on fairness and equality
lawyer	a person trained in legal matters – often working as a solicitor, a barrister or a judge
legislation	the process of making laws: and the laws that a state has
magistrate	a person with little or no legal training who is given authority to enforce the law in minor cases
manslaughter	unlawful killing where there was no prior intention to kill: murder is killing 'with malice aforethought' – i.e. 'having previously decided to do it'
multi-cultural	the attempt to enable people to celebrate and share their many different backgrounds and cultures
nationalist	strongly attached to your own country
negligence	carelessness
Old Bailey	the central criminal court in the Strand in London where many famous cases have been heard
oppression	when a state aggressively and violently prevents some or all of its members from being free citizens
Parliament	the primary law-making body in the United Kingdom – made up of elected representatives of all the people
plaintiff	in civil law – the person making a complaint
precedent	an earlier decision made by a court which is presented as a reason for making the same decision in another case
probation officer	someone who supervises and supports convicted criminals in the community
prosecution	the attempt to prove that a defendant has committed the crime
prosecutor	the person or organization bringing the prosecution
Queen's Counsel	a senior barrister, abbreviated as QC
rehabilitation	the attempt to help criminals stop offending
remand	the period of time between being charged with an offence and being tried in court. Remand may be on bail or in custody.
rights	in human rights theory those things we need to live a properly human life (such as right to life, to education, to healthcare and so on)
rule of law	the strong use of the legal system to ensure good order – this may enable freedom, it may be oppressive
sanction	something promised, threatened or done in an attempt to persuade someone to act in a particular way
sentence	the punishment decided by a court for an offence
small claims court	a fairly informal court in which people can discuss their complaints about one another and be helped to come to an agreement
social worker	someone who works for a social services department specially trained to help people in difficulties
solicitor	a legal official who, rather like a GP for people who are ill, is the first port of call for people who need the advice and help of a lawyer
tort	in civil law – a wrong someone causes someone else, for which there may be compensation or damages
tribunals	groups of people appointed to listen to evidence and make decisions
vendetta	a quarrel going on for a long time, often leading to violence and killing
verdict	the decision of a court: 'guilty' or 'not guilty' are verdicts

INDEX

Titles in the *Citizen's Guide* series include:

Hardback   0 431 14493 1

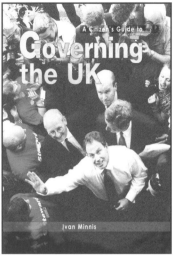

Hardback   0 431 14492 3

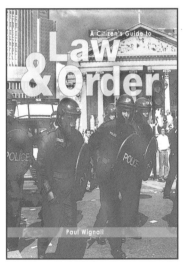

Hardback   0 431 14495 8

Hardback   0 431 14491 5

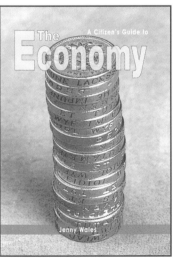

Hardback   0 431 14494 X

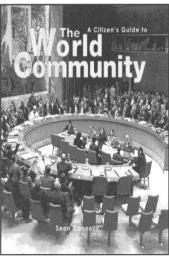

Hardback   0 431 14490 7

Find out about the other titles in this series on our website www.heinemann.co.uk/library